IN LIFE

THERE ARE

MANY

THINGS

In Life There Are Many Things

Poems

Lucy Wainger

BLACK LAWRENCE
PRESS

Black
Lawrence
Press

www.blacklawrence.com

Executive Editor: Diane Goettel
Chapbook Editors: Kit Frick & Lisa Fay Coutley
Book and Cover Design: Zoe Norvell
Cover Art: "NlucYCy" by Elena Perez

Published 2023 by Black Lawrence Press.
Printed in the United States.

"its not even time until it was"
—William Faulkner, *The Sound and the Fury*

CONTENTS

Dark is a bathroom
I go home to.
    I spend lots of time
in bathrooms—

    chasing thoughts with
my tongue: it bends,
    makes a ring. In life,
there are many things.

    When I eat birds
I spit them out; bees,
    I swallow. These are the rules.
The sun is zero,

    the moon a smaller
zero—facts I memorize
    the sound of, like a song
with no words. During recess,

    I hum. I sit
on the bench—I don't know
    how to play—
I sit on one end and then

    I slide to the other.
In the cafeteria, I eat

oranges and their juice spurts
like boys. That is what hands

are for: wiping mouths.
I want to sing. I want to break
        something but I think
that is a wrong thing to want.

        These are the rules.
They look funny
        from behind. I am terrible
at staying where I am put.

        In class, we learn about zero
and the ocean
        and gravity, the string
that ties them together—

        a long string the air moves, like my hair
when I play. I wish I had
        the biggest pair of scissors
in the world. I have

so many questions, but
        I don't know
how to catch them. I have
        this body—

residue—and I don't know what
        left it.

NEIGHBORHOOD

The sky is blue again and all the knees around me
bend. I look. A big red cut shaped like a fingernail,
a mouth starting to open. Litter on the sidewalks
glittering like candy. A big red mouth bleeding
cherry candy, dull gray smoke. Grown-up arms
wrap around me and grown-up legs start running
all in the same direction: away. We run all the way up
to the streets with the numbers on them. We move
all the way up to a street with a number on it, but
then we have to move again, and again, and I get lice
so we cut off my hair and soak it in oil. Ugly gray
crayon I drag off the edge of the paper to show
the smoke, only that's not really what it looked like.
I learn that Daddy didn't wake up until the second
plane hit. He went into the living room and there weren't
any windows, just different kinds of dust. He gives me
so much candy my mouth goes dull as a knife.
I get so hungry I have to eat until it hurts. I eat slabs
of dead things and look for the raw part, the softest
pink, my favorite color, but then I start dressing
like a boy. This is the kind of thing teachers call
a story: Daddy didn't wake up until the second plane hit.
But he never wakes up when the sun is out, anyway.
He stays awake all night at his machine, its dull gray
glow. At night he cooks me dead things, cooks away
all the pink. When we finally get to move back home,
there are windows. The furniture is all blood orange

and cherry red. Across the street, instead of two big
buildings, there is one big hole, which they are covering
with metal, which is stupid. Sometimes I like it here.
How nobody knows where I live. I am a very small thing
and I am so good at slipping past fat pale crowds of people
with cameras. I am hard to surprise and easy to fool
because I know that so many things are normal.
My hair is long like a girl's and my clothes are ugly
like a boy's, so my body is just right. I can't help it,
I have to pick the stupid scabs until they bleed cherry
candy, salty caramel. I sleep through the sun
and its dull gray glow, and my alarm goes off
but I don't wake up. I can't help it, I hate going
to the playground—I don't know how to move my arms.
I don't know how to move my legs, my open mouth.

THE OTHERS

1.

The pool drinks them
and I am unswerving,
I keep to tile edges.
I've been

hateful lately.
They are chlorinated.
They are a party
with pale legs
I want to tear open.

2.

I keep to the edges of things.
I think I am something
primordial; I ooze.
My bathing suit

bunches and stinks, the campus
grows thick with goose shit.
They are one big block
of stinking yellow money.
I am a block, a block.

3.

The pool drinks them
with its greedy tile mouth.
Beauty is a story
for little kids

and I am big.
No one should have to
be born. The hallway tightens
around them, either I can look
or look away.

4.

We change out of bathing suits.
I watch their pale legs and fingernails.
They are sheets of blank paper
I want to soak with ink.

I towel my hair, my clattering
limbs, the evil places
where my body folds. I watch
the windows shudder and warp
and the hallway tighten, tighten

GIRL BEFORE A MIRROR

A sphinx is a woman made
of parts that are not woman:
lionheart, wings for skin,
scales falling from the spine and city ruins.
Bomb-leveled.
Maybe that's the crossroads' riddle—
how to shake your head and smile when you're standing
in a crater,
towers quivering, then
collapsing, pipes gurgling at your feet,
bleeding out
your reflection. These things do have a way
of getting under the skin. Making the blood whir.
As if somewhere inside your body
you forgot to turn off the stove.
Your heartbeat: *And yet. And yet.*
Thick ridges
of scar tissue catching and releasing the light
like glowing fish—in an abstract sense, you know
this is called a wrist,
mottled spider: a hand. Broad planes of flesh
retreating into a thicket of hair. Somewhere
your name.

I perch upon the roof and send
paper planes to the roof across
the street—scrape the sky
like a knee, streak of dried blood
so close I want to lick it
and swallow. I was born
in this city, which means
I do not know how to live
in this city, this island
of mirrors and windows
mimicking mirrors, sending
my own face back to me
when I walk past. I was born here:
I know what to do when the building
burns, begins to choke
with smoke, but I can't be sure
my body knows how to jump.
From my perch, it is easy to believe
the city spread before me
is no more than what a subway map
makes easily navigable. I know
where I am going and I know
how I will get there, my hands
buried in jacket pockets.
Surround me with water
I can't drink and other islands
I can't touch—bridges stitching

a wet wound. At the river, I lean
as far over the railing as my body will go
to see my own face in green water.
I want to shatter it and surface.

Your eyes widen because you're the deer—
hair, hooves, proud antlers and animal heart now
pounding in place, blood-beat, fear-fixed, eyes

widening, widen—look at you: you're the deer
and the car careening toward the deer, you're the deer
and the high beams spotlighting the deer, dust motes

stupid in the shaft of light, the sudden driver
who sees too late to stop, and why pick a body?
a scene?, you're the on-screen crash and the crowd

watching the screen, body with a hundred eyes
and a hundred hands and the split-second
impulse between them but I can't help it—

every deer needs a car, every crash a camera,
every camera an audience and a camera catching
the audience. Their hands sit still and their eyes

don't shut, their hands come together but their eyes
won't shut: you're the car and the body in the car,
the road and the body in the car on the road

fading to black in both directions before
the careening beam of light cuts you in half,
catches animals as if with a trap, a steel jaw clamped

around your own cloven foot, your eyes straining
for a way out of the road, out of the body on the screen
we watch in the dark, holding our eyes in our hands,

insatiable, sick with fear and fake butter. No way
to say it and see, no way to say it and still
mean it a moment later, a mile away—a degree

removed—what can I tell you?, arms wide as they'll go,
eyes widening still, my body a body I see from
my seat, my body a body I leave on the road?

MONOLOGUE FROM THE WINGS

Their voices harden under spotlight
and the audience's gaze,

their costumes tight as bodies.
In this script, energy crisis is imminent—

the backdrop an orgy of traffic
light colors. Took weeks to paint.

Now I finger the edge of the canvas, fray it.
See the top and the bottom, unpainted. No one

is supposed to see. I am full of bad love,
which is allowed.

Soon the lights will go out in the script.
Soon the lights will go out on the stage.

I will need help with the ropes,
the curtain is too heavy to draw

alone. I remember someone
here—grin too bright

in the dark—said my name
like a question and I did not answer.

MURDER SCENE DIPTYCH

I. VICTIM

You check the rearview mirror, let your eyes
begin to pack your final box: the town
you'll soon have left. The life you left without,
you flatten into imagery—concise
and easy to recall: the seagulls' screech;
the smell of flapping fins and failing gills;
squat buildings, always ruined and rebuilt,
now pickled as they are. As what you'll keep.
The rearview mirror town you've left is small
and so is everyone left living there.
Caress who you remember. Smother. Pack
each body-mess into the name you'd call
across the street, or down the creaking stairs,
if you were there to call. If you went back.

II. UNSUB

I find you in the bathroom, meet the eyes
of your reflection's fleshy smear: a map
to lead me nowhere. You turn on the tap.
This rest stop is as empty as surprise.
I want to know how animals can tell
each other from each other. What's the sign?
What holds the holes, the hairs, the harried smile
together—architecture? Force of will?

I straddle you. I wedge my thumbs into
the sockets of your sight; I knife, I pare
away the skin, the cartilage, the blood
of so much bruise, and what lies underneath?
A silent blankness, hard and white. No word
from you, not even where you might've gone.

TEEN WOLF

Here is the story where language
can't save you: rabid adolescent
scrabbling across the wet asphalt

of your high school's parking lot, chasing
or being chased by some imaginary
monster—real as the bright taunt

of moon bouncing off your bared teeth,
ridiculous claws. Ridiculous moon.
Impossible sun: an assignment you'll do tomorrow

if you live until tomorrow—if you blink
awake in the woods, maybe, body bruised
like ripe fruit, bits of other animals

stuck between your teeth, artifacts
of unimaginable hunger. Right now
it is imaginable. Right now

you are running because you can't stop
running, because the thing behind you
or ahead of you won't stop running—a monster

which, like you, was a myth
and then was not, did not exist until it did,
until the night cracked in half, sank

its jagged edge into your thigh
and renamed you. A werewolf
is someone for whom language is binary:

howl vs. silence. The rest
is petty detail—crabgrass fur
and the sweatiest hunger, an ache

arching upward, away from the earth
with its fragile claims and faulty
evidence, contracts broken

like human bones. Here is the story
where language can't save you,
where every word bursts out of its shape

to howl at a singular moon. In this story,
the asphalt is wet, your parents still think
you're asleep in bed, and the present

is a thing chasing you through the dark,
a streaking blur you won't have a name for
until after you've gotten away.

NOTES FOR *OEDIPUS REX* ESSAY

1.

"In the beginning" was a thing
that was also another thing:

cast son as knife, bed, king
of the stricken city, symptom

and impossible wound—the riddle
we know the answer to

until the answer ages. I was fifteen
when I began this essay.

Four-legged girl, furious with plague,
certain it'd kill me before

I finished the play—

2.

A locked door and then bile-colored carpet.
Cranberry juice frozen in its carton. Reconstituted eggs.
Roommate sleeping through breakfast, then lunch.
Daily schedule written on the whiteboard.
Hallway lined with payphones. Ringing now—
it's not time to answer. TV behind its plexiglass screen.

Pain on a scale of zero to ten (none, worst imaginable).
How are you feeling? How are you doing today?
The book you have to read for school: a metal grate
over your eyes. Each word shut and locked.
Phone again. Somebody answer it, answer—

    3.

In the margin, my teacher's handwriting is a pile of blue ribbons:
"What would it look like to live inside the in-between?" I cut class
to rest my forehead on his office desk. It is the time of year school
starts and ends in the dark, and in this exact moment, I am the
oldest I have ever been. I possess a most imperious knowledge:
what cannot kill me now never will. Contrapositive: what will kill
me might as well. My teacher furrows, shakes his head, but he
cannot tell me why. Why can't—

    4.

At the crossroads, a king and a girl
of fur and scale, tail and teeth:

any point at which to stand
and not decide, forms of life

streaming outward as if
to reveal themselves. What now

without eyes, what new seeing
splits open? No myth

remembers this, the crossroads
crossed again, the girl asking

how?, How?, and her wings—

     5.

The cut across your left cheekbone, flaking now.
The burns on your right hip, blistering now.
Oil puddling in the creases of your eyes, nose, lips.
Blood pressure cuff around your upper arm, softening
like a human hand. The book you're holding—
shitty Dover edition. Text passing through you
like water. You can die because you know everything now.
You're sure of it. The taste of red vomit
and liquid charcoal. You know what happens next.
When the phone rings, I'll answer it for you.
Look outside. Look, it's starting to snow.

That round red sound drops ripe from your mouth,
rouses the memory: a frantic gesture toward
the thing on the table between us—how your laugh burst
and scattered like shards of a teacup. *What else
do you remember?* A sense of loss, maybe.
Blooms bleeding out, layers of bright paint
muddying, never dry. Someone was already repeating it—
that sound. *And the thing on the table?*
I want to look at the world without needing to take
a bite from it, this wildness my mouth makes,
chewing and chewing. I don't know
what time it is. I don't remember what I saw,
only what it came to mean. *Incessant grass.*
The smell of mud and rain. You told me
we are a story—one on the run from its author.
Tell it to me, then. Tell me again.

IN THIS POEM, A GOAT'S HEAD HANGS
FROM A TREE BRANCH

and sings. A boy cuts the goat's heart from its body
and plants it. Weeks later, a herd of bumblebees

bubbles out of the dirt. The boy's wristwatch, stopped
since autumn, starts ticking again. Several miles away,

it's autumn. Rain congeals into snow. Apple trees grow
oranges while nobody's watching, while everyone's

asleep. Hundreds of miles away, in the hospital, a girl
dies slowly, spitting at her doctors' hands. Months later,

she goes home. *I don't know how it happened. I didn't mean
to survive.* A bee stings the back of the boy's left knee.

THE ROAD TO ROME

I swallowed fifty aspirin, vomited—red as the August streets of Rome.
My mother held my hand as she did when we walked the streets of Rome.

A century earlier, no one watched Quentin Compson drown himself
in Mississippi—a place that lives forever, like ancient Greece or Rome.

My first day, one of the boys explained why he'd tried to kill his brother.
Doctors don't want to understand. How I had to. How Remus needed Rome.

In group therapy, the new girl told an old story, her voice burnt.
We listened as if playing violin, absorbing the distant heat of Rome.

I remember metal grates over the windows, the smell of disinfectant.
Tragedy is secondhand, wrote Faulkner: not the hour but the story of Rome.

An old friend asks me how I made it out—how I wake up, get to school.
I can't answer his hoarse voice. I can't explain the geography of Rome.

I slump in the hallway, knees to chest, while our class reads Plath's "Tulips."
When I was a child, health was a place as far as here from Rome.

In the hospital, I told my mother I could never forgive her my birth.
In August, I will be an adult—lined with ruins, like the city of Rome.

The child in me thrashes, spits. My teacher names her for the drowned boy.
All questions beg this answer, Quentin insists: *All roads lead to Rome.*

L'HÔPITAL'S RULE

I have never been to the hospital
in Georgia. In Georgia, there are rules.
I have learned a few of them, although
I have not lived here long. Although
I have not lived there for awhile
now, I remember a few rules:
no pens. No underwire bras. No physical
contact. Of course, the rules might differ
in the adult ward, or in Georgia. In Georgia,
I have never tried to divide my body
by zero. My hair has grown
long and purple, a river in the hands
of the girl I love. In the hospital,
I soaked my fingers in the water fountain.
I eyed an electrical socket, sought to honor
my deformities. I do not know the rules
of mathematics in Georgia, but I remember
how it feels to reach and grasp nothing.
Of course, the rules can change. The rule
is change. Is crossed out, then clear
as a horizon. Of course, the horizon
shimmers: limit of the body's
jurisdiction. I do not rule the body
of the girl I love, nor the body
of the girl I was, who is the city
I go home to, which is an island,
which I am always forgetting.

Unlike the girl I love, the girl I was
does not touch me, for she has
no body, my body her derivative—
feeble shade, pale purple flame—
the rate at which she does not change
while the girl I love learns the rules
of hospitals in Georgia.

A VIEW FROM THE BRIDGE

RED HOOK

New York is a slaughterhouse
we keep from bleeding out: spend long blue days
dragging sacks of coffee beans from ships,
uniform, until someone
drops their cargo and burlap splits
and spills out a harvest.
This is how we learn about accident.

SICILY

Everywhere, statues; everywhere, bones
turning into statues. Take this seriously.
We crouch in the river, feel it flood the cracks
in our cracked feet. We have so many
bodies—so many configurations
of bodies. The water runs through each.

RED HOOK

Our grandparents came here for two or
three good reasons. One: streetlights—

the safety afforded to those who settle
beneath blotted-out stars. Two: the dream
of American mothers rocking American sons to sleep,
the end of the song twisting into breakwater.
Three—

SICILY

Everyone here is either a lawyer or a priest,
has a voice to speak disaster
and a law to follow home. We know
how this works: the way sentences finish
themselves; the way the story ends
as brutal light, too bright
to look at, and we look. We look.

RED HOOK

This is how we learn to use our hands.
This is how we hold New York: grip
gentle, as if it might not cut open
our palms. The workday ends
and we get a drink, quiet, the last light
streaming through the glass. Last light
streaming through the glass—enters, bends.

PHYSICAL EDUCATION

We fold into the sixth-floor gymnasium like wings / along a spine, opening the windows, / every window. We ask to open / every window and the light falls / in, drip / drop, click clack, / basketballs pound the gessoed floorboards. / Tenderize. / The heart is also / a kind of meat, by which / I mean it can be eaten. / We have thirty-four mouths. Nearly twice as many hands. / Birds fall in through / every open window, like light / streams through translucent hands / streams through glasses of water / bodies of water. Our spines unfreezing, refreezing, all the vertebrae / rearranged, all the light refracted, / all the birds dripping / feathers, our hands folded / wings, fists / basketballs, skin / stretched canvas, mouths open / notebooks and we need / to eat. / The thing they don't tell you / about refraction / is you have a body all the time.

NOTES FOR *ENDGAME* ESSAY

CLOV   What is there to keep me here?
HAMM   The dialogue.
       SAMUEL BECKETT

Between us, two backpacks, books piled like kindling
on the back corner cafe table—ours whenever we can claim it:

whenever it's not too crowded here, the second floor of the grocery store
where, on winter afternoons, everyone gathers to do homework and drugs,

to stay warm. Lately we've been living here. Lately all my English essays
have led me to the same conclusion: a kind of silence

that has nothing to do with the frozen Hudson, or forgetting, or family
    dinners
we won't go home for, a kind of silence it takes so many tries to get to:

weeks of class, a lot of really bad poems; albums you will always associate
with the R train—morning commute—and I will always associate

with winter afternoons. I gulp black coffee, you buy an entire
rotisserie chicken for dinner, and between us, two backpacks, the essay

I won't finish, the air your voice swims through. What do we know except
the snow piling up on the sidewalks has fallen over so many other islands,

what the fuck do we know except we read this book and liked it.

WANTING TO LIVE

The best nights of my small life happened
by accident. We drank beer, went nowhere
and I had never been so loved by boys before.
Never since. Going to college taught me

I am not ambitious.
Things rarely go where I mean to throw them.
The great project of my life, for instance, was
to kill myself; look how that turned out.

A failure, slick and slow. In the meantime, leaves
became discarded wrappers, boys I loved
applied to college, I learned things
I now forget. How little you can carry on your back.

I didn't mean to want to live, those school nights
we had nowhere to go except not home, but
I couldn't help it. I loved those boys. Liked living
in the stain where I'd spilled.

comes wave after wave after wave the derivative and harvest, the myrtle tops of sandstorms and milk glasses, apple, horse and song, list, listen, light leaks from the spaces between the bubbles—call it foam—tender pocket of *yes yes yes* call it flesh—eat tonight and you'll still have to eat tomorrow, eat tonight and it still won't be over—eat tonight: peaches bloom even in the dark, as wet as a girl—hands and feet, horse and song, the same hole bandaged over and over, not a wound but its absence—a sum of histories—the nights colliding like marbles, and if there is an end then it's too dark to see, if there is an end it's too bright to see, hands folding, unfolding, and you, Scheherazade!, milky goddess of recursion, best DJ in the city, you spin records, spin heads, cross legs and cross deserts, and always pause just moments before he

This chapbook takes its epigraph from William Faulkner's novel *The Sound and the Fury* (1929). The lack of apostrophe in "its" is not a typo.

"In this poem, a goat's head hangs from a tree branch" takes its titular image from Brigit Pegeen Kelly's poem "Song" (1994).

"The Road to Rome" is for Theo Danzig. It references a character and takes a line from *The Sound and the Fury*.

"A View from the Bridge" takes its epigraph from Arthur Miller's play *A View from the Bridge* (1955).

"Notes for *Endgame* Essay" takes its epigraph from Samuel Beckett's play *Endgame* (1957).

ACKNOWLEDGEMENTS

Thank you to the editors of the journals in which some of these poems first appeared, often in different forms: *Bayou Magazine, The Boiler, DIAGRAM, The Margins, Nashville Review, Passages North, Peach Mag, POETRY, Puerto del Sol, Redivider, The Rupture, SOFTBLOW, Vinyl,* and *Winter Tangerine.*

Thank you to the teachers who helped shape some of these poems or otherwise supported this chapbook: Jericho Brown, Sumita Chakraborty, Heather Christle, Peter Gizzi, Lucia LoTempio, Elizabeth Onusko, and William Wright.

Enormous thanks to the team at Black Lawrence Press for bringing this chapbook into existence. Shout out to Elena Perez for drawing the cover art.

Thank you to Dr. Nash, EG, the Stuy English department, my family, and all my beautiful friends.

IAN JACOBS

LUCY WAINGER grew up in New York City. She's currently an MFA candidate at UMass Amherst, where she teaches composition and creative writing. *In Life There Are Many Things* is her first chapbook.